Creepy-Crawlies

Victoria Munson

WINDMILL
BOOKS
™

Published in 2019 by Windmill Books,
an Imprint of Rosen Publishing
29 East 21st Street, New York, NY 10010

Editor: Victoria Brooker
Book Design: Elaine Wilkinson
Photo Credits:
Alamy/The Wildlife Studio 10; iStockphoto.com 11
eli_asenova; Shutterstock.com: cover centre Vitalili
Hulai; tr (stag beetle) alslutsky; t (honey bees) Peter
Waters; bl (swallowtail butterfly caterpillar) Anest; br
(snail) EsHanPhot; (ladybirds) irin-k; 2, rpt 16 Marek
Velechovsky; 3b, rpt 13 goran cakmazovic; 3t Arto
Hakola; 3b Zdenek Kubik; 4 mikeledray; 5 Suede
Chen; 7t Bruce MacQueen; 7b Karel Gallas; 8 Pavel
Krasensky; 9t Sue Robinson; 9b Stephan Morris;
10b StevenRussellSmithPhotos; 10t Bachkova
Natalia; 11t Ger Bosma Photos; 11b Henrik Larsson;
12r colin Robert varndell; 12l Kuttelvaserova
Stuchelova; 13t goran cakmazovic; 13b Greg Gillies;
15t ChiccoDodiFC; 14 Hermit crab; 15b IanRedding;
16b Marek Velechovsky; 16t Chris Moody; 17
IanRedding; 18b Ezume Images; 18t Steve Byland;
19t Philippova Anastasia; 19 Arno van Dulmen;
20 kingfisher; 20t David Peter Ryan; 21 Maryna
Pleshkun; 22r Vectomart; 22l benchart;
23 NotionPic

Cataloging-in-Publication Data

Names: Munson, Victoria.
Title: Creepy-crawlies / Victoria Munson.
Description: New York : Windmill Books, 2019. |
Series: My first book of nature | Includes glossary
and index.
Identifiers: LCCN ISBN 9781508196082 (pbk.)
| ISBN 9781508196075 (library bound) | ISBN
9781508196099 (6 pack)
Subjects: LCSH: Insects--Juvenile literature.
Classification: LCC QL467.2 M86 2019 | DDC 595.7-
-dc23

Manufactured in the United States of America

CPSIA Compliance Information: Batch #BS18WM:
For Further Information contact Rosen Publishing,
New York, New York at 1-800-237-9932

Contents

What Is a Creepy-Crawly?

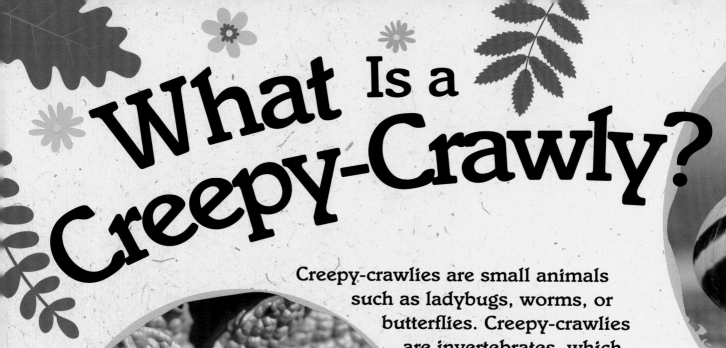

Creepy-crawlies are small animals such as ladybugs, worms, or butterflies. Creepy-crawlies are invertebrates, which means animals without a backbone.

Creepy-crawlies do not have a skeleton in their bodies, so their bodies are soft and bendy.

To protect their bodies, some creepy-crawlies, such as snails, have a hard shell.

Many creepy-crawlies use antennae, hairs, or even feet to taste, smell, and touch. Snails use antennae to smell with.

Butterflies use their feet to taste with.

Creepy-crawlies can be found in many different habitats, from backyards and forests to ponds and lakes.

Some creepy-crawlies are also called bugs.

Beetles

Ladybugs are a type of beetle. Many ladybugs have red wings with black spots. The bright red color warns predators that it will taste horrible.

Some ladybugs are yellow, orange, or black. Some ladybugs have stripes or patches.

Ladybugs can beat their wings 85 times a second.

Soldier beetles are orangey red. Their bright color is a warning to predators to stay away.

Soldier beetles are also called leatherwing beetles because of their soft wings.

Stag beetles eat mostly sap from plants.

Stag beetles get their name from their large jaws, which look like a stag deer's antlers.

Stag beetles use their jaws to fight other stag beetles.

Pond Creepy-Crawlies

Backswimmers swim upside-down. While moving, their legs look like the oars on a rowboat.

They are also known as water boatman.

Backswimmers are carnivores, which means they eat other animals, such as insects, fish, and tadpoles.

Pond skaters are small bugs that can walk on water.

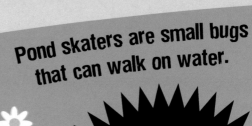

They have tiny hairs on their feet that repel water and allow them to "skate" on the surface.

Dragonflies can be many different colors, from red, brown, and orange to bright green or blue.

Look for dragonflies hovering over the top of ponds, looking for food.

Dragonflies have large eyes that help them detect prey.

Butterflies

Peacock butterflies get their name from the yellow and blue eyespots on their wings.

These spots look like the markings on a peacock bird.

In the winter, peacock butterflies hibernate in hollow trees and sheds.

Red Admiral butterflies have black and red patterns on their wings.

Red Admirals like to suck juices from rotting fruit.

Large and small white butterflies look similar, but the large is much bigger than the other.

Large and small white butterflies are also known as cabbage whites because the caterpillars love to eat cabbages and sprouts.

Caterpillars are long and worm-like, with six legs. In the spring and summer, caterpillars turn into butterflies.

Wasps and Bees

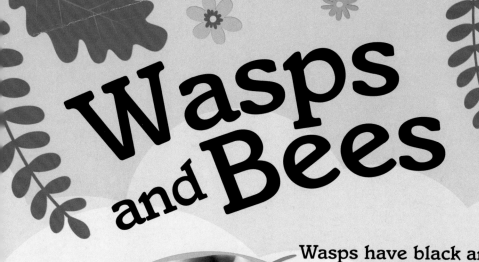

Wasps have black and yellow stripes. Large groups of wasps live together in nests.

The nests are usually in holes in the ground.

There can be up to 2,000 wasps in one nest.

You can tell hornets from wasps because hornets have brown and yellow stripes, not black and yellow. Hornets are also twice as big.

Honeybees have brown-black bodies with orangey-yellow bands.

Honey bees sting when they feel threatened, but afterwards, they die. Wasps can sting again and again.

Buff-tailed bumblees pollinate raspberries and blueberries.

Buff-tailed bumblebees have black and yellow stripes with a white tail.

Seashore Creepy-Crawlies

Hermit crabs don't have their own shell. They live inside the empty shell of other animals, such as periwinkles and whelks.

A crab's soft body is protected in a shell.

Hard, red pincers stick out of the shell, helping them to move and catch food.

Mussels have blue oval shells. Mussel shells are tightly closed out of the water, but underwater they open to take in food.

With their tentacles hidden away, beadlet anemones look like jelly-shaped blobs attached to rocks.

Beadlet anemones can be red, green, or brown. They use their tentacles to sting prey and drag it into their body to eat.

One beadlet anemone can up to 192 tacles.

Centipedes, Millipedes, and Woodlice

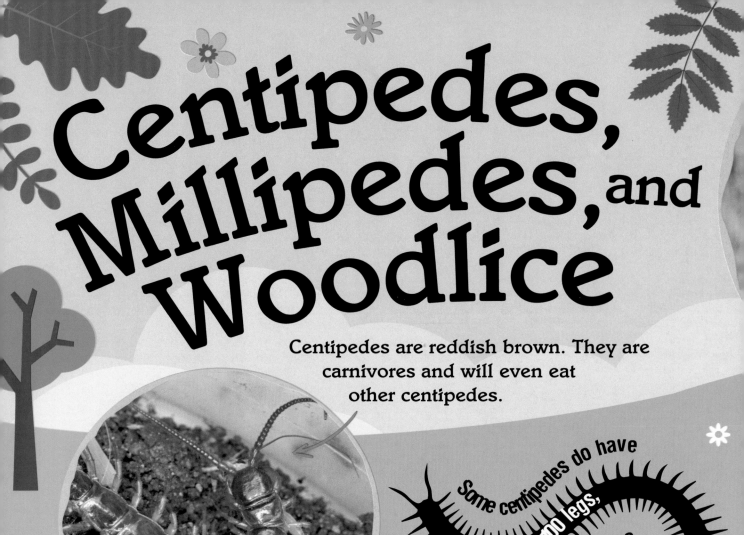

Centipedes are reddish brown. They are carnivores and will even eat other centipedes.

Some centipedes do have over 100 legs, but some have only 30 legs.

Centipedes live in the soil, hidden beneath rocks, logs, or tree bark.

Millipedes have between 40 and 400 legs. Some millipedes release a smelly liquid to keep predators away.

When millipedes are frightened, they roll up into a ball.

This millipede is called a white-legged snake millipede.

Woodlice have a hard outer shell called an exoskeleton.

Woodlice have 14 legs and two antennae. Look for woodlice under rocks or logs.

Woodlice are eaten by centipedes, spiders, and toads.

Slugs, Snails, and Spiders

Garden slugs grow to 1.5 inches (4 cm) long.

Slugs have two pairs of tentacles. One pair is used for seeing and smelling. The other pair is for feeling and tasting.

Slugs prefer wet or damp weather because they will dry out in very hot weather.

Snails live in dark, damp places, such as under plants and near soil.

As snails get older, their shells get thicker.

Garden spiders have eight legs and a hard outer skeleton. They are carnivores, which means they eat meat.

Spiders spin webs to catch their prey.

Garden spiders have a large white cross on their backs.

Ants, Earwigs, and Worms

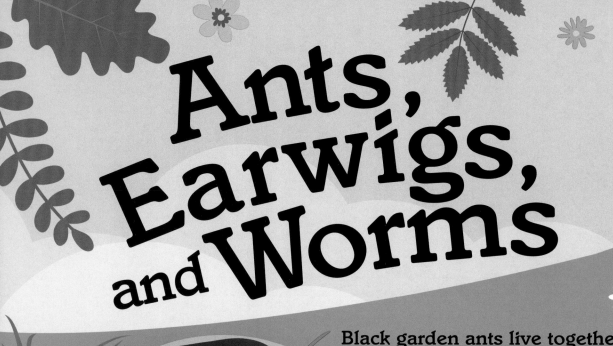

Black garden ants live together in huge nests on the ground.

A black ant nest can contain more than 5,000 ants.

Ant nests can be found in sidewalks, in between bricks, or in soil.

Ants come into houses to look for sweet foods, such as jam or sugar.

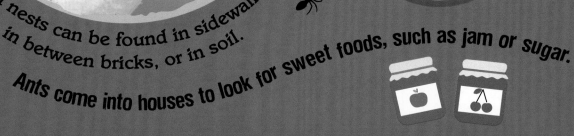

Earwigs have pincers at the end of their body. Earwigs are mostly nocturnal, coming out to feed at night.

They hide under flowerpots, logs, and stones.

Earwigs got their name because of their ear-shaped wings, although they rarely fly.

Earthworms live in the soil. Their soft bodies are made up of segments. They have a mouth, but they don't have eyes or a nose.

Use a magnifying glass to look at the hairs on a worm's skin.

Earthworms have many predators, including birds, hedgehogs, and foxes.

21

Where to Find Creepy-Crawlies

Many creepy-crawlies hibernate or spend the winter as eggs, so the best time to look for them is in late spring or summer. Look for creepy-crawlies in these habitats.

1

Under a log
Woodlice, earwigs

2

In the soil
Worms, ants, centipedes, millipedes

3

In gardens and parks
Caterpillars, butterflies,
bumblebees, honeybees,
beetles

4

In undergrowth
Snails, slugs

5

Around ponds
Backswimmers, pond
skaters, dragonflies

How many
creepy-crawlies can you
find? If you move any
creepy-crawlies from
their habitat, always put
them back where you
found them.

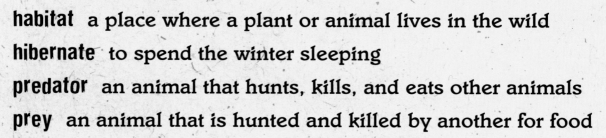

Glossary and Index

habitat a place where a plant or animal lives in the wild

hibernate to spend the winter sleeping

predator an animal that hunts, kills, and eats other animals

prey an animal that is hunted and killed by another for food